EXTREME WEATHER

BLIZZARDS

NorwoodHouse Press

JACK WILLIAMS

Cataloging-in-Publication Data

Names: Williams, Jack.
Title: Blizzards / Jack WIlliams.
Description: Buffalo, NY : Norwood House Press, 2026. | Series: Extreme weather | Includes glossary and index.
Identifiers: ISBN 9781978576834 (pbk.) | ISBN 9781978576841 (library bound) | ISBN 9781978576858 (ebook)
Subjects: LCSH: Blizzards--Juvenile literature.
Classification: LCC QC926.37 W555 2026 | DDC 363.34925--dc23

Published in 2026 by
Norwood House Press
2544 Clinton Street
Buffalo, NY 14224

Designer: Rhea Magaro
Editor: Kim Thompson

Photo credits: Cover, p1. Studio, Nick Starichenko/Shutterstock.com; p. 5 justkgoomm/Shutterstock.com; p. 7 Piaffe Photography/Shutterstock.com; p. 8 Leonid Ikan/Shutterstock.com; p. 9 Lizard/Shutterstock.com; p. 10 Bilanol/Shutterstock.com; p. 11 jokerpro/Shutterstock.com; p. 12 mariakray/Shutterstock.com; p. 13 PBouman/Shutterstock.com; p. 15 vitec/Shutterstock.com; p. 16 pio3/Shutterstock.com; p. 19 Rokas Tenys/Shutterstock.com; p. 20 Skripnik Olga/Shutterstock.com

Printed in the United States of America

CPSIA compliance information: Batch #CWNHP26: For further information contact Norwood House Press at 1-800-237-9932.

TABLE OF CONTENTS

WATCH OUT!

Snow falls.

Wind whips.

It is hard to see what is in front of you.

Watch out! It is a **blizzard**.

WHAT IS A BLIZZARD?

A blizzard is a powerful winter storm.

Snow falls for at least three hours.

Strong winds blow.

The temperature is **freezing**. High in the sky, storm clouds form. Snow falls from the clouds.

Warm air quickly rises over cold air. This causes mighty winds.

Blizzard winds can blow faster than a cheetah can run!

WHY ARE BLIZZARDS DANGEROUS?

Snow piles up in **drifts**. It can block roads. It can make roofs **collapse**.

High winds can knock down power lines.

Blowing snow fills the air. This is called a **whiteout**.

Walkers cannot see where they are going.

Drivers cannot see the road.

Cold temperatures are dangerous for people outside. They can get **frostbite**. They can get **hypothermia**.

HOW TO STAY SAFE

Watch the weather **forecast**.

A blizzard warning means that a blizzard could form.

Weather
Blizzard
0°
Chances of rain
Humidity
Wind

Gather supplies.

If the power goes out, keep warm with coats and blankets.

Stay inside until the storm is over.

GLOSSARY

blizzard (BLIZ-urd): a severe snowstorm with strong winds

collapse (kuh-LAPS): to fall down suddenly and completely

drifts (drifts): piles of snow created by the wind

forecast (FOR-kast): a report that tells what the weather will be like in the future

freezing (FREE-zing): below the temperature at which water freezes into ice; below 32 degrees Fahrenheit (0 degrees Celsius)

frostbite (FRAWST-bite): a condition in which very cold temperatures damage a person's skin, especially on the fingers, toes, ears, or nose

hypothermia (hye-puh-THUR-mee-uh): a condition in which a person's body temperature has become dangerously low

snow (snoh): white crystals of ice that fall from the sky when the water vapor inside clouds freezes

whiteout (WITE-out): a situation in which blowing snow limits a person's ability to see very far

wind (wind): moving air that you can feel when it blows

THINKING QUESTIONS

1. When do blizzards happen?
2. What causes strong winds to blow?
3. How can blizzards damage buildings?
4. Why are blizzards dangerous for people?
5. Where should you be during a blizzard?

INDEX

ABOUT THE AUTHOR

Jack Williams is curious about all things in nature, especially the weather! He checks the weather forecast every day. He used to be a police officer, so he knows how important it is to watch out for danger and stay safe.